LAUGH-OUT-LOUD JOKES

LAUGH-OUT-LOUD BUG JOKES

BY LEONA FOWLER

WINDMILL BOOKS

Published in 2026 by Windmill Books, an Imprint of Rosen Publishing
2544 Clinton St., Buffalo, NY 14224

First Edition

Editor: Caitie McAneney
Book Design: Claire Zimmermann

Photo Credits: Cover, p.1 (child smiling) suriyachan/Shutterstock.com; series art (paper texture) OanaGherghe2/Shutterstock.com; series art (illustrations) cover, pp. 6, 8, 16, 18, 20 (bee), 22, 23 (illustrations) Look_Studio/Shutterstock.com; series art (illustrations) pp. 4, 10, 12, 14, 16, 18, 20 (dragonfly) Nadzin/Shutterstock.com; p. 5 Vinicius R. Souza/Shutterstock.com; p. 7 (left) A Turton/Shutterstock.com, (right) Baronb/Shutterstock.com; p. 9 (left) slonme/Shutterstock.com, (right) chinahbzyg/Shutterstock.com; p. 11 olko1975/Shutterstock.com; p. 13 AMR Captures/Shutterstock.com; p. 15 frank60/Shutterstock.com; p. 17 Adeel Ahmed photos/Shutterstock.com; p. 19 Steidi/Shutterstock.com; p. 21 Stephen A. Waycott/Shutterstock.com.

Library of Congress Cataloging-in-Publication Data

Names: Fowler, Leona, author.
Title: Laugh-out-loud bug jokes / Leona Fowler.
Description: Buffalo : Windmill Books, 2026. | Series: Laugh-out-loud jokes
| Includes index.
Identifiers: LCCN 2025001911 (print) | LCCN 2025001912 (ebook) | ISBN 9781538399088 (library binding) | ISBN 9781538399071 (paperback) | ISBN 9781538399095 (ebook)
Subjects: LCSH: Insects–Juvenile humor. | Wit and humor, Juvenile. | LCGFT: Humor.
Classification: LCC PN6231.I56 F69 2026 (print) | LCC PN6231.I56 (ebook) | DDC 818/.602–dc23/eng/20250128
LC record available at https://lccn.loc.gov/2025001911
LC ebook record available at https://lccn.loc.gov/2025001912

Manufactured in the United States of America

CPSIA Compliance Information: Batch #CSWM26. For further information, contact Rosen Publishing at 1-800-237-9932

CONTENTS

Words in the glossary appear in **bold** the first time they are used in the text.

FUN WITH FLIES!

How's a spider like a baseball player?

BOTH CAN CATCH A FLY!

What do you call a bug that lost its voice?

A HOARSE FLY.

What do fireflies say to one another?

"YOU GLOW, GIRL!"

What has two wheels and flies?

A TRASH CAN!

FUN FACT!

Horse flies grow up to 1 inch (2.5 cm) long! Female horse flies can give painful bites to animals and people.

BEE SERIOUS!

How do bees style their hair?

WITH HONEY COMBS!

Do bees drive to work?

NO, THEY TAKE THE BUZZ.

What do bees take with them when it rains?

THEIR YELLOW JACKETS.

What do bees say when they return to their hive?

"HONEY, I'M HOME!"

FUN FACT!

Earth is home to more than 20,000 bee **species**! These small insects are sometimes **confused** with other stinging insects, such as yellow jackets and hornets.

honey bees

yellow jackets

LAUGH WITH LADYBUGS

What do you call a musical group of ladybugs?

THE BEATLES!

Why did the ladybug come out of hiding?

SHE'D BEEN SPOTTED.

Why do ladybugs like improv?

THEY'RE GOOD AT WINGING IT!

What do ladybugs use for decorations?

LARVA LAMPS.

FUN FACT!

Some ladybug species have larvae that look like tiny alligators! They are black, spotted, and spiky.

larvae

MOSQUITO MADNESS

Why wasn't the bat invited to the mosquito party?

HE WAS A REAL BUZZ KILL.

Why shouldn't you cross a mosquito?

THEY'RE ALWAYS OUT FOR BLOOD.

Did you hear the story about the mosquito?

I'M ITCHING TO TELL YOU!

Knock knock.

WHO'S THERE? Amos.

AMOS WHO? A mosquito!

FUN FACT!

Mosquitos may be small, but they kill more people than any other animal on Earth by spreading **disease.**

BUTTERFLY BITS

Why didn't the butterfly go to the dance?

IT WAS A MOTHBALL!

Have you ever seen cheese run?

NOPE, BUT I'VE SEEN BUTTERFLY!

Did you hear about the power-hungry butterfly?

HE WAS A MONARCH.

Why shouldn't you eat caterpillars?

YOU'LL GET BUTTERFLIES IN YOUR STOMACH!

FUN FACT!

North American monarch butterflies **migrate** up to 2,500 miles (4,023 km) away each year!

FEELING ANTSY

How many ants live in an apartment?

TEN ANTS!

What did the hurt ant say?

"SOMEBODY CALL AN ANT-BULANCE!"

What's the largest ant on Earth?

THE ELEPH-ANT.

Why don't ants get sick?

THEY HAVE ANTY BODIES!

FUN FACT!

Ants can use **chemical** messages, called pheromones, to talk to one another. They are great at teamwork!

SILLY SPIDERS

What's a spider's favorite vegetable?

CORN ON THE COBWEB.

What do spiders do on the weekend?

GO FLY FISHING.

What do you call spiders on their honeymoon?

NEWLYWEBS.

What job is best for a spider?

WEB DESIGN.

FUN FACT!

Spider webs are made of a strong silk, and each has its own special design.

WHAT'S THE BUZZ?

What do you call a bee on your doorbell?

A HUMDINGER!

What did the confused wasp ask himself?

"TO BEE OR NOT TO BEE?"

Are wasps the same as bees?

NO, THEY'RE JUST WANNA-BEES.

What kind of haircuts do hornets get?

BUZZ CUTS.

FUN FACT!

There are thousands of wasp species on Earth! Most live alone and do not sting people. Hornets and yellow jackets are known to sting.

BUG TALK

What did the dog say to the flea?

"QUIT BUGGING ME!"

What did the fly say to cheer his friend up?

"YOU'RE GNAT ALONE."

What did the frog say to the waiter at the diner?

"I'LL HAVE THE FRENCH FLIES."

What did the hornet say to the bee?

"BUZZ OFF!"

FUN FACT!

Gnats are small flies that often fly in large clouds. Some are biting and some are nonbiting.

GLOSSARY

chemical: Matter that can be mixed with other matter to cause changes.

confused: To be misunderstood as something else. Also, to misunderstand.

design: Making the plans for something.

disease: Illness.

hoarse: Rough or harsh in sound.

improv: Acting without a plan or script.

larvae: Bugs in an early life stage that have a wormlike form. The singular form is "larva."

migrate: To move to warmer or colder places for a season.

monarch: A ruler who has total power.

species: A group of plants or animals that are all the same kind.

FOR MORE INFORMATION

BOOKS

Clasky, Leonard. *Let's Tell Jokes About Bees*. Buffalo, NY: Windmill Books, 2023.

McClure, Leigh. *Rhyme Time with Ants!* Buffalo, NY: Gareth Stevens Publishing, 2024.

WEBSITES

10 Facts About Honeybees!
www.natgeokids.com/au/discover/animals/insects/honey-bees/
Learn some fun facts about honeybees to go with your favorite bee jokes!

Butterflies
www.ducksters.com/animals/butterfly.php
Learn all about butterflies, including their life cycle and cool features.

Publisher's note to educators and parents: Our editors have carefully reviewed these websites to ensure that they are suitable for students. Many websites change frequently, however, and we cannot guarantee that a site's future contents will continue to meet our high standards of quality and educational value. Be advised that students should be closely supervised whenever they access the internet.

INDEX